THE LAST BOUQET
and
Other Poems

Also by Gerald N. Battle

LITTLEST FIDDLER AT THE OPRY

SIMON PETER, THE BOY WHO BECAME A FISHERMAN

GIDEON, THE BOY WHO LEARNED TO LEAD

LUKE, THE BOY WHO WANTED TO MAKE PEOPLE WELL

ARMED WITH LOVE, THE STORIES OF THE DISCIPLES

THE LAST BOUQET

and

Other Poems

Gerald N. Battle

NORMAN S. BERG, PUBLISHER

"Sellanraa," Dunwoody, Georgia.

1973

This is an edition of 750 copies of which 700 copies are for sale.

ISBN 0-910220-49-2

To Mary

Contents

Gerald Battle; The Last Bouqet

The Last Bouqet

You were April
With a silver pipe,
Playing a frolicsome tune.
You were May
In a new green cloak,
Counting the gay umbrellas.
You were
A young, warm June,
Waiting under the magnolia trees.
You were the fanciful lady
The wind sings to,
As she swishes along
The shadowy lawns.
That's how I remember you.

An Hour Past Forever

Genius is a flame
Leaping chimney high;
Cleverness is smoke
Rising to the sky;
Wit's a cedar log
Sending sparks that fly;
Wisdom is a chimney
Tall and deep and wide;
Love's a sturdy fireplace,
Holding all inside.

Flame, and smoke, and cedar,
Giving fireside glow;
Chimney tall and fireplace wide
Keeping warmth inside;
Some things last a long time,
Reflecting work's endeavour;
Love lasts longer than a lifetime—
Lasts an hour past forever.

Footprints

So shall we go
Our separate ways,
With but a backward glance
For former days.
Our small diverging paths
Shall know,
Nothing of past.
If our footsteps are more slow;
Our ways
Shall be more wise.
And, knowing more,
We will forget surprise,
At things
We thought absurdly gay.
Thus shall it be,
Along the way.
Day comes—night, dawn,
Each of us will see,
Pause for an instant,
And go on.

Last Act

Gone!
Lightly tossed
And air-caught,
Swifting
Far away,
Like
Slanting rain.
Some little movement
Of your hand;
Some word I spoke
Before,
I gave it
To my mind,
To see.
Sign-posts
For a turning,
Swift over-shoulder glances,
One brief glimpse
Of doorway light.
And then dark,
Like a guillotine blow
Descending—
Swiftly, swiftly
On a thousand
Insignificant things;
That mattered
So little.
So little as life,
They mattered.

San Francisco By Night

Walking!
Rain-slick ornaments
In city streets.
The magic sesame
To golden treasures,
Glass enclosed,
Only a look away,
Separated by eternity.
Dragons lurk the streets;
I walk still
The windmill land.

Love Song

Tomorrow;
Hours bewitched,
Pools in which,
Reflections will be cast,
Skies where clouds,
May pass;
Roads that lead
To anywhere.
Bright balloons
Rise and drift,
Trespassers in space;
Lovers climbing toward the sun,
Running in the race,
That can't be won;
And all our tomorrows
Pushed eagerly in play,
To reclaim,
A single yesterday.

The Left Side of My Heart Limps A Little

I cannot know
An infinite glory
Of exquisite pain
At having lost you.
I will not smile
And wish you luck,
When you tell me
There is another.
When you leave me,
I will sit
In this room,
Where so often,
We have been together.
Here I will stay,
Feeling no pain,
Knowing no sorrow,
Or bitterness;
But simply loving you.

Do you think
Because you close the door,
And walk away,
I shall stop?
Do you think one word,
Or many words,
Can shut everything away
In a neat, little box;

With a tip of my hat
And a smile,
To ribbon the package with?

I shall stay here
In this room,
Loving you until
Something inside says
You are gone . . . quite gone.
Then I shall go out
And love another.

Reprise

Ask the winds, my love.
To whisper what I cannot tell.
Speak to the stars,
Woo them with the smile
You never gave,
But sold so well.
They'll ignite your fierce heart's
Cold fuel,
And if you find it still amusing
To be cruel,
Whistle through the mist,
For memory to haunt
The dreams of some dull worshiper,
You can no longer taunt.

Smoke Rings

When careless laughter
Has no wings;
When castles-in-air
Tarnish from dreams to desire;
When my quick jest dulls;
And your heart no longer sings;
When quiet pleasures
Seem neither brave nor gay;
Let's take the turning
For another way;
Our love has been
A small clear light.
It will not last
Through one dark night.

Interlude

I saw her lips
Curve in a smile.
I heard a banal phrase
Expressing gaiety.
I laughed
And wondered,
If she knew.
And then I saw,
That in her heart,
She was laughing, too.

Oak Room Charade

I often wonder,
When wondering seems
The fashion,
What men would do
Were it not for ladies
Who stir
Our hearts and passions.
And often I think,
While wondering thus,
On men and women,
And passions;
Why the three
Go hand in hand,
Or hand in glove,
If you like.
And as I ponder,
She smiles,
And her eyes promise more.
As I muster my charm,
My dreams skip through the door,
On somebody else's arm.

Toast

Life is a winging wine,
Drain the cup.
Don't sip it slowly;
Life is a singing wine,
Flooding the blood with song,
Drain the cup.
Leave for thin-faced bitter lads,
The latter wine,
Those dregs of cautious days.
Stand undaunted,
Drain the cup!

Only Because I Love You

My dear I wonder
If t'would mar
The clear, unblemished
Surface sheen,
To know exactly
What you are?
Would it enhance
The beauty seen,
Add new lustre to the star?
These line, I fear,
Are idly penned;
For what is truth,
Where beauty's kenned?
And so for the surface
Hang a wreath.
One seldom cares
For the underneath.

Breakfast Table Samurai

The words
Were rapier thrusts,
That cut
So deep, so clean,
The wounds,
Were scarcely seen.
I smiled,
In satisfaction
At my skill;
Until—until,
I saw
The thin red line;
And knew;
The heart that bled,
Was mine.

Always The Wind

This then is all!
The end,
The blotting out
Of past small intimacies.
But I shall ever dream,
And rain must fall;
Always the wind
Will blow your hair;
Our parting
Cannot mist away the stars,
Or throw a veil
About the moon.
We are as shadows,
You and I,
From whose depths
Have gone faint echoes,
Dying low,
But singing still.
Lovers die
When love is gone;
But their songs,
Greet each new dawn.

Magic

Found a four-leaf clover,
Had good fortune all the day;
Heard a Mocker singing,
Heard him say,
Be gay, be gay.
Watched a sunset blush the sky,
Heard the west wind
Hurry, skurry by.
Saw a yellow moon
Climb a thousand ladders high,
As seven solemn oak trees
Waved goodbye

Three Things

Three things
Bring heaven near:
Cedar logs
Burning in my own fireplace;
A cardinal in the snow;
The smile of her
I hold most dear.

Mourn not the lost,
And one-time golden day;
For fame is fable,
Fortune far away.
Three things
Bring heaven near.

Wreath

A Flame grew tired of burning;
Those who knew
The rightful place,
For shadowed clay,
Placed the dark ashes here.
Saintlier souls leave heel marks
On the grass.
The few who loved her
Still dare,
To look at the sunset;
A flame burns there.

Touch Me And I Will Know

Touch me and I will know!
Fragile, whispered words
Shatter in the understanding.
Only touch me and I will know.

All the promises of sunrise and moon-glow,
And Summer grass, and Winter snow,
And Autumn night, and all of Spring,
Are in the coolness of your fingers,
Touch me and I will know!

Sing me no songs; I will not hear,
Tell me no words; I dare not listen.
The ending is so surely clear,
I hide from the challenge of my heart;
Not brave enough to stay; not bold enough to go.
Touch me and I will know!

Girl In The Blue Kimona

Happy thought,
Pleasant dream,
Silver fish
In sparkling stream,
Beautiful painting,
Superb cuisine,
Ah so!
But not tonight,
No;
Arigato,
Not tonight, Miyoko.

Riddle

Was he dark,
Was he fair?
I do not know,
Or care.
I only know
He fought, and lost,
But striving,
Gave his best.
And by this very effort
Crowned himself
With laurel leaves,
Which only I could see.
I won, with careless ease,
The silver cup.
And who was victor,
I or he?

Friend

We saw each other
With no awareness,
Preconceived or otherwise
Indicative of what
Later came about.
I say
We saw each other;
And that
Was all it was,
Mere seeing.
And yet there was,
In each of us,
Something,
Which made the other,
Pause and say a word,
Offer a cigarette;
Comment on the weather;
Until the awkward moment
Grew into
An hour's talk.
The updraft caught
Our casual acquaintanceship,
And fanned it into flame,
And friendship.
We drank coffee,
Pushing salt and pepper shakers
Across the table,
While we argued
Over things,

We did not wholly understand.
So it began;
We found our points-of-view
Enough alike,
And yet apart,
To let each share,
Almost unwillingly,
Portions of thought and mind
Usually withheld.
Once in an auto crash,
We missed, by a moment
Too sudden death.
Remembering these things,
I think it well to say,
We never quite agreed
On anything;
Except that,
The separate worlds,
In which we lived
Were better,
For having known
The warmth
Of each other's smile;
Or the sharp regret
At disapproval,
Frowning from a face
We'd come to know,
And look upon,
As something special.

The Road To Rome

We are the death throwers,
The crumblers of cities,
The destroyers of towns.
Look at us as we pass by,
Stare at our grimed beard-stubbled faces.
Death and destruction ride with us;
We are their grim messengers.

You, old man, sitting in the shambles of your
    home,
Why do you beg for bread?
Your life is nearly gone,
Why do you want more of it?
And you, child of starvation,
Why do you cry for food?
Is it well to grow up in this world?

Wave to us as we pass by,
We the hollow-eyed ones,
The gaunt and the lean—
Smile at us as we go,
And remember the food we share,
The candy we tossed to the chidren—
Wave to us as we pass by.

Behind us come others
Who build up all that we destroy,
Others with food and comfort and peace,
And a new world

To offer for the old.
You will be grateful to them,
But think kindly, too, of us, if you can.

We are the flame throwers,
The weary and dirty ones,
Ours the job without joy.
Remember, too, the white crosses
Where the poppies grow
Among the wheat—
Some of us sleep there.

Slowly goes the old world,
Quickly comes the new.
Smile at us as we go by,
And tend the fields with care
Where poppies and white crosses
Grow among the wheat—
Some of us sleep there.

Give Us The World

We will come back
To the farms, to the factories,
To the tree-shaded small town streets,
To the crowded city streets,
We will come marching,
All of us.

All of us?
Yes, all of us.
Those who sleep now
In far off places,
Only rest,
While we, their comrades.
Journey home;
They will come back.

You, who greet us
From the town-hall steps,
Make no speeches,
Promise no promises;
Build no monuments.
Give us the world
We never had before,
And dedicate it
To our sons,
That they need never sleep,
As others do,
Lulled by the waves
Slowly slapping
Against a far off shore.

Homecoming

Sun in the sky,
Trees lovely as before,
Birds singing,
White chickens in the yard,
Bittersweet memories surround me,
The postman makes his round,
People passing by.
Why doesn't it all stop,
Or whistles shriek,
And sirens scream.
Even the gate sags sadly;
He was always going to fix it,
But he never did.
The paper boy tosses his wares;
He does not know;
None of the people know.
I want to shout to them:
"Listen, all death's been here."

Souvenirs

Tattered letters,
In careless disarray;
Whimsical cards,
From some special day;
Campaign ribbons,
With battle stars;
Fading reminders,
Of ancient scars.
A small bronze medal,
Symbol of daring;
An old class ring,
Too small for wearing.
Yesterday's hopes,
Joys and fears;
Tucked away in a corner,
Today's souvenirs.

Suddenly Spring Came

It was winter when I saw you
Standing in the snow;
It was winter when I saw you,
Hair like midnight
Lips like flame.
You glanced my way
And smiled.
Suddenly Spring came.

Skies were dreary,
Sullen clouds had kidnapped sun.
My heart was tired of beating,
All my gay songs,
Left unsung.
Then you came
Around the corner,
Quick steps,
Spelling rhythm's name.
Then you came
Around the corner,
Suddenly Spring came.

Where Lovers Walk The Blue Begins

Vapor trails, heaven turned;
Cedars, lonely proud,
Hill sentinels,
Watchful through the night.
Remembered forest pool,
Faithful,
To a small endeavour.
Paper pilgrim, sun-faced;
Darting dipping,
Falling, climbing,
Bravely climbing,
Bravely climbing,
Dancing toward forever.
Fragile dream,
String-halted.

Coronation

Panting lovers,
Eager to be blind,
Building pedestals to place
Their love upon.
I never visioned one
For you.

Eager lads
Storm out to greet,
The invitation of your eyes;
And what you freely give,
They call deceit.

Some foolish hero
Weaves a halo for your head.
I alone know,
You need a crown to wear.

I could not offer this,
You thought I did not care.
The wonder is,
I did.

I had no jewels
For your hair,
And there was nothing else,
For us to share.

I Knocked On Your Heart

I knocked on your heart
And couldn't get in.
Called out your name,
And heard no reply.
No songs left to sing,
No place left to hide,
I wandered in sadness
To smell all the flowers.
Time turned into madness,
A clock without hours.
What do you seek,
When there's nothing to find?
How can you leap
The gulfs of the mind?
I came back at last
To begin a new beginning,
Hopeless, alas,
With no thought of winning.
I knocked on your heart,
You opened it wide.
I called out your name,
You whispered mine.
So, late in the game,
Without reason or rhyme,
I knocked on your heart
And found you were mine.

Shadows On The Floor

Outside the window,
Evening stalks in solemn gloom.
The flashing neon sunset,
Knocks upon my door.
Every lost and lonely thought
Sits with me in my room,
Cast their shadows on the floor.

Against the window brush the snowflakes,
Softly falling.
But my mind, sees only waves,
That break upon a distant shore,
Hears, a well-remembered voice,
Gently calling.
And my wonder turns to ashes,
In the shadows on the floor.

The arrows of the mind
Hit targets seldom aimed for;
And the anxious heart beats wildly,
With each footstep in the hall.

Love, longing to be duped,
Hears a thousand knocks upon the door;
Banishes the mocking silence,
In a frenzy of recall.

I gaze upon the picture
I have looked upon before;
And all my sudden hopes desert me
In the shadows on the floor.

Whirlwind Of Tomorrow

In the whirlwind of tomorrow,
Can we find a promise there.
Will we forget the older sorrow,
Finding hope and not despair.

Will love ever be the password
Which unlocks the crystal door.
Will bitterness be banished—
A silent note unheard.
Can I borrow from tomorrow,
Just one moment more.

In the whirlwind of tomorrow,
Can the hoped-for dreams come true.
Does each bow own a second arrow,
Is there hope for me, for you.

Whirlwind of tomorrow,
Prize beyond the gambler's dare,
Can we find a sun still shining,
Build a plan of new designing,
For a love which we can share.

White-Manteled Days

There must be gray skies
And trees,
Standing black
Against the gray;
Waving gaunt
Uncovered branches,
Windward.
There must be
White-manteled days,
When gray and white and black
Suffice the longing,
Our hearts feel
For rich colors,
Touched by the sun.
So we must sing
The winter song,
Before we climb
To some high balcony alone,
And listen
For Spring's serenade.
So has it ever been;
So shall it always be:
Gray sky, white world,
The lonely tree,
The winter song,
Then Spring.

Growing Old In Manhattan

One must look down
On a well-lighted town;
At it's glimmering, shimmering
Big town light.
One must walk
Through the streets
At night;
Steal a glimpse
Of the moon,
As a yellow kite.
See the yellow-kite moon
Look down,
And frown.
One must feel
The hugeness,
And the crowd.
And hate it,
And love it,
And laugh out loud.
Laugh at it's lights,
Laugh at it's moon;
Sigh that you've come,
And leave too soon.

All My Worldly Goods

Maine beaches in November,
A mountain top,
One star,
Forsythia blossoms in December,
The lightning-splintered tree,
Rain on country roads.

All The Trees Are Green

We laughed at tomorrows,
Cried 'folly' to our dreams;
We were young and without sorrows,
All the trees were green!

Ours were the mountains, ours alone to climb,
Fear was only fancy, suddenly turned mean,
There was no enemy named time,
And all the trees were green!

We climbed one mountain peak,
Fashioned fame from yesterday, it seemed,
Found scorned tomorrows, all we had left to seek,
But all the trees were green!

Slowly we grew wise, taught by the years,
Inept students of the changing scene,
Masters of a desperate wisdom, bought with tears,
And still, and still—all the trees are green!

Winter Song

Can we begin
To know?
Can we find ways
To go—
Each to each,
Reaching to
One star?
Is there
A dream,
Within a dream?
A heart,
Which beats,
Unevenly in time;
With rhythms wild—
Too wild
For fancy's flight;
Too hidden in reality
For love's delight.
Can we begin
To know?
Or reach for a star,
And find one hand?

Compensation

If you had only known me then,
If you had only known me when
I was one-and-twenty!

If I had only known you then,
If I had only known you when,
You were turning twenty!

But the years that passed unseen,
And the unshared time between,
Make these moments we are sharing
Sweeter than they might have been.
For if discretion slows our daring,
So has love replaced, just caring.

We Blew Out The Stars

We mocked at the moon
And blew out the stars,
Then whistled in darkness,
As we fingered our scars.
Wild, wild—how wild we've been
Trying to regain a child's delight.
Gone, gone—we lose the scene,
And quickly fades from sight
What might have been.
Aimlessly we run
On the treadmill of our making,
In an endless maze of yearning,
All the golden days forsaking,
Looking for a turning—
For a turning we can find,
Where forgiveness lasts forever,
And the heart still rules the mind.

Someday

Someday
I'll bring them to you,
Spread them on the hearth,
Before your chair;
The simple things,
I am not brave enough
To show you now;
The melodies
My heart has sung
And stored away,
The thoughts I know,
But cannot tell you of
Today.
Someday,
I'll grow bold enough
To spread them on the hearth
Before your chair.

So Long

So long as you still live
And I still live
My heart shall hoard the long-remembered things
We two made part of one another.
The sun in my life,
The warm color of joy,
Quiet evening shadows on the lawn,
The clear, crisp autumn days,
The vivid whip and tang
Of crowded city streets,
The simple dignity
Of Sunday in a town we knew and loved,
The fun of dancing to a favorite tune . . .
The quiet glory of your smile,
The sharp pain of saying good-by
For perhaps a little while,
Perhaps forever.
So long as you still live
And I still live
We'll get together.
Till then—
My heart remembers.

White Plumes

I did not understand,
So, when your eyes
Said no,
I smiled
And clasped your hand.
Too young,
Too immature,
You said.

Since last I walked
In woods with you,
I've lived
A thousand years—or two.
Since last,
We watched
A thrush take air,
White plumes
Have come—into my hair.

White plumes
You sighed for
Long ago;
I wear them now,
And sing a bolder song.
I come again,
No longer young,
To say
Be gay—be gray
With me.